POCKET PICTORIAL

Cotswolds

Stephen Dorey

MYRIAD

LONDON

Cheltenham

Early settlements at Cheltenham were noted for their peaceful atmosphere and quiet prosperity but the discovery of a spring, in what is now Cheltenham Ladies' College, in 1716 gave rise to a sudden burst of popularity and affluence. During the Regency period Cheltenham Spa rivalled Bath in its splendour. Handel and Dr Samuel Johnson were among the town's notable visitors but the Spa reached the pinnacle of its success with the five-week visit of King George III in 1788. Much of the architecture and layout of today's town dates from this period. In the 19th century the passing trade of the Spa was replaced by permanent residents, often, it is said, retired colonial officers with liver complaints!

Regency Cheltenham

The Regency passion for horse-racing is maintained at Cheltenham racecourse, situated at Prestbury Park to the north of the town, home to the annual Cheltenham Festival and Cheltenham Gold Cup. Cheltenham retains many of its fine Regency features such as spacious

squares, crescents, terraces, promenades and beautifully laid out formal gardens. These are to be found on either side of the striking tree-lined Promenade. The source of Cheltenham's wealth can be seen in its neo-Classical Pittville Pump Room. As well as racing, Cheltenham hosts several major festivals each year, including those devoted to music, science and literature.

Sudeley Castle Sudeley Castle has had a rather chequered history. There was a castle on the site in Norman times but this was replaced by Sir Thomas Boteler during the Wars of the Roses. In the Tudor period the castle became the home of Katherine Parr, the last wife of Henry VIII, and in the Civil War it was Prince Rupert's headquarters. Sudeley then fell into disrepair until it was acquired by the Dent family in 1837. Extensive restorations were carried out under Lady Emma Dent. Katherine Parr had married Thomas Seymour after the death of Henry VIII but she later died in childbirth. Her marble tomb, designed by Sir Gilbert Scott, is in St Mary's church, close to the castle.

Winchcombe The unspoilt town of Winchcombe is tucked away into the Cotswold edge and is sheltered on three sides by pleasantly wooded hills. Winchcombe was one of the seats of the Saxon kings of Mercia and was later a county town until it was absorbed by Gloucestershire. In the Middle Ages its abbey was a place of pilgrimage for followers of the martyred St Kenelm. The abbey has now completely disappeared. Most of the buildings that distinguish the town today are largely the legacy of the Cotswold wool trade. The town also benefited from its proximity to Sudeley Castle when the castle was the seat of great magnates and a host for royal visits.

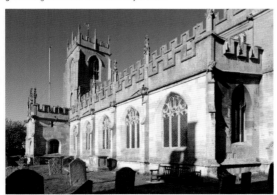

Crickley Hill From the slopes of Crickley Hill there are fine views across the Severn Vale plus many areas of archaeological, geological and ecological interest in its country park. Crickley Hill is the site of a hill fort that was inhabited since Neolithic times. Extensive excavations in the area have revealed that the settlement was often refortified and may have been the site of ancient conflicts. On the Iron Age part of the site is a defensive wall standing 12ft high but this has been reburied beneath the soil to preserve it. A modern visitors' centre provides information on all aspects of the area.

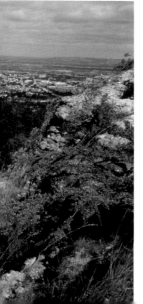

Withington The manor of Withington was formerly held by the bishops of Worcester and several of its buildings date back to the 15th century. The Mill Inn lives up to its name and has the river Coln running through its gardens, although no water wheel is present. At the centre of the village is a well-preserved Norman church. The exterior has many Norman features including a solid tower and splendid south doorway but unfortunately the interior was rather over-enthusiastically cleaned up during the Victorian period. A large Roman villa once stood in the area and a mosaic pavement from it is now in the British Museum.

Leckhampton Despite becoming a suburb of Cheltenham, Leckhampton has managed to maintain its own character and charm. The old village grew up around Leckhampton Court (now a Sue Ryder Hospice) and its associated church, and both buildings are still very much in evidence today. The church has an elegant tower and spire and preserves interesting brasses and memorials. At the end of the 18th century Brandon Trye, a local landowner, developed quarries in the area and built a horse-drawn railway to transport stone into Cheltenham. One particularly hard pillar of rock was left by the quarrymen and is now known as the Devil's Chimney.

Naunton The village of Naunton lies in the upper Windrush valley and can often be seen in its entirety from nearby hills. The village has been a centre for sheep-rearing since it became monastic land in the Middle Ages. This long history of animal husbandry means that this part of the Windrush valley is home to flowers found only on unimproved limestone pasture. In particular cowslips can be found in the spring, whilst yellow rattle and orchids adorn the fields in summer. The other industry in Naunton was the production of stone roofing slates; at one time 30,000 a week were dug from thin stone seams in nearby mines. The church has an imposing Perpendicular tower complete with pinnacles and gargoyles.

Temple Guiting Situated on the river Windrush not far from Guiting Power, the Temple part of the name of this village comes from the 12th century when the manor was owned by the Knights Templar. St Mary's church in Temple Guiting is built in an unusual combination of medieval and Georgian classical styles. Temple Guiting manor house was described by Pevsner as "one of the finest, if not the very best of the small Cotswold Tudor manor houses".

Gloucester Built mainly on the eastern bank of the river Severn and dating back to Roman times, Gloucester is sheltered by the Cotswolds to the east, by the Forest of Dean to the west, while the Malvern Hills protect the city from the north-west. Gloucester's cathedral has its origins in an abbey founded in 681; it is the burial place of King Edward II. In the Middle Ages it was a centre for pilgrimage. Gloucester's long and prosperous history as a trading centre, inland port and spa can be glimpsed in the many fine buildings and churches that adorn the city.

Cirencester This was an important city during the Roman era and stood at the junction of three major roads: the Fosse Way, the Ermin Way and Akeman Street. The only visible remains of the Roman city in modern Cirencester are part of the old town wall and a large turf-covered amphitheatre. The town's prosperity in the Middle Ages was aided by the presence of a large abbey and it eventually grew to pre-eminence in the wool trade. At the centre of Cirencester is its marketplace which even today retains a great deal of the atmosphere of a busy prosperous Cotswold wool town. Rising above the marketplace is the 162ft (49m) high Perpendicular tower of its church – the largest in Gloucestershire.

Barnsley Barnsley village is chiefly noted for Barnsley House Garden. Barnsley House itself dates from 1697 when it was built for a local landowner, Brereton Bouchier. It later became a parsonage but came to fame when Rosemary Verey took over its gardens in the 1950s. She created a variety of garden types including an 18th century herb garden, a knot garden, a laburnum walk, a temple with pool and a vegetable garden.

The Ampneys This small group of villages, as their name suggests, lie on the Ampney Brook. Each has its own church and both were thriving communities during the Middle Ages. Down Ampney (above) was the birthplace in 1872 of composer Ralph Vaughan Williams; his father was the local vicar. The original parish of Ampney St Mary has disappeared making its church seem isolated. The present Ampney St Mary was formerly known as the hamlet of Ashbrook. The church of St Mary is a small Norman structure that still preserves many fascinating original features such as a carved lintel and medieval wall paintings. The church of the Holy Rood (an Anglo-Saxon word for cross) gives Ampney Crucis its name and there is a rare 15th-century cross in its grounds. This was hidden from 17th-century Puritans by being walled up inside the building.

Bibury This picturesque village dates back to Saxon times but the bulk of Bibury owes its existence to the 17th-century wool trade. Pretty Arlington Row is a terrace of weavers' cottages.

Chedworth Opposite the ancient Seven Tuns Inn a spring emerges from a wall. The church retains some Norman features but it has been sensitively added to over the centuries.

Northleach One of the most important Cotswold wool towns in the Middle Ages, Northleach's heyday as a medieval trading centre can still be glimpsed in its market square and half-timbered buildings. The most obvious legacy of the wool trade is the church of St Peter and St Paul. This was largely rebuilt in the Perpendicular style in the 15th century and is a magnificent example of the style and period. The pinnacled south porch is said to be without equal in England and the tower combines both elegance and strength.

The Duntisbournes

The four villages that bear the name Duntisbourne are strung out in a line along the Dun Brook. They are Duntisbourne Abbots, Duntisbourne Leer, Duntisbourne Rouse and Middle Duntisbourne. Only Duntisbourne Abbots and Duntisbourne Rouse have churches. Today, Duntisbourne Leer is little more than a couple of farmhouses by a ford. The more interesting of the churches is the tiny church of Saint Michael in Duntisbourne Rouse. Overlooking the Dunt

valley, it has a Saxon nave and, because of the sloping ground, a small crypt chapel beneath the Norman chancel; this is unusual in such a small church. It was designated a Grade 1 listed building in 1958.

Snowshill There have been settlements near Snowshill since the Bronze Age. A barrow nearby contained a famous collection of weapons now in the British Museum. Snowshill was owned by Winchcombe Abbey from 821 until the Dissolution of the Monasteries when it was given to King Henry VIII's wife Katherine Parr. The main part of the current Snowshill manor house dates from around 1500. In 1919 the almost derelict building was bought and restored by Charles Paget Wade, who needed somewhere to present his diverse collection of 22,000 examples of craftsmanship, amassed between 1900 and 1951.

Stow-on-the-Wold Stow has the dubious distinction of being the highest town, at 800ft (244m), in the Cotswolds. A popular rhyme begins, "Stow-on-the-Wold, where the wind blows cold"; the shape of its unusual market square is in part dictated by the need for stallholders to be protected from the wind. Despite its position, Stow-on-the-Wold has been a thriving market town since at least 1107 when it received its first royal charter. By the 15th century there were two annual fairs and Daniel Defoe reported the sale of 20,000 sheep in a single day. In later years Stow-on-the-Wold became famous for its horse fairs, but nowadays the only horses at the two charter fairs, one held in May and in one in October, are likely to be on the merry-go-rounds. Stow-on-the Wold is also the site of one of the last major battles of the Civil War. A royalist march on Oxford with 3,000 men was thwarted by Cromwellian forces and 1,000 men were imprisoned in the church.

Upper Slaughter Although it sounds bloodthirsty, the name "Slaughter" is probably derived from the Old English word *slohtre* meaning slough or boggy place. The two villages that bear the name are both beautifully situated on the upper reaches of the river Eye. They are only half a mile away from each other, but they are very different in character.

Lower Slaughter The manor house here dates back to 1650 when it was built for Valentine Strong, the owner of a quarry at Little Barrington. The house has been remodelled since its construction but its grounds preserve one of the largest dovecotes in Gloucestershire. Several simply built footbridges span the river Eye in Lower Slaughter. The two villages lie less than a mile apart on the banks of the river Eye. Lower Slaughter tends to be more photogenic and attracts a greater number of visitors than its near neighbour.

Moreton-in-Marsh The position of Moreton on the Fosse Way and other transportation routes accounts for its existence and prosperity. It was on the main coaching route between London, Oxford, Worcester and Hereford. When coaching declined the town moved on to railways; the Stratford-Moreton Tramway – a forerunner of the railway – opened in 1826 and was one of the earliest in the country.

A mainline service arrived in 1843 and the line between London, Oxford and Worcester was opened in 1853. As a centre for travellers Moreton-in-Marsh is well provided with inns one of which, the 16th-century White Hart (Royal) Hotel, was used by Charles I during the Civil War. It is also said to be haunted. The Curfew Tower on the corner of Oxford Street still has its original 1633 curfew bell hanging in it; the bell was in daily use until 1860. Chastleton House, three miles south-east of the town, is a fine Jacobean manor house which still contains much of its original furniture; it is now run by the National Trust. Two miles from Moreton-in-Marsh is the Four Shires Stone, a Cotswold stone pillar that marks the coming together of the four old county boundaries of Gloucestershire, Worcestershire, Oxfordshire and Warwickshire.

Blockley This was one of the first villages in England to produce its own electricity, thanks to the power of the Blockley Brook. In previous centuries the brook provided the energy for corn mills, silk throwers and even wood saws. Six mills once operated in the village although only one is still open; the beautiful Mill Dene garden has been created around another. Parts of the church date from the Norman period but the tower was added in 1725.

Saintbury This small village is ranged along the side of Saintbury Hill. The name Saintbury probably refers to a Saxon holy man called Cada who built a small cell nearby. The Norman church still preserves some fragments of a former Saxon building. The village itself features a fine cross which stands at the crossroads to the north of the village. The lower part dates from the 15th century whilst the Maltese cross and sundial were added in 1848.

Chipping Campden The word "chipping" relates to an Old English word meaning market and it was as a wool and cattle market that the village first grew up. The many fine houses in the town are evidence of its successful trading past. Grevel House was built for William Grevel in about 1380 and features striking Perpendicular-style two-storey windows. The

market hall was constructed in 1627 and was intended for the sale of cheese, butter and poultry in a period when the wool trade was in decline. The pretty row of almshouses just below St James' church dates from 1612; they originally cost £1,000 and are still used today to house 12 Campden pensioners. St James' church is a significant local landmark. It is built in the Perpendicular style and features a 15th-century pinnacled tower.

Broadway Regarded by many as the finest large village in the Cotswolds, Broadway, as its name suggests, has a wide main street; the village was once an important staging post on the London to Worcester route. A new turnpike road was opened in 1736 and at one time seven coaches passed through the village each day. Many of the fine buildings along Broadway's main street began their lives as inns to serve passing trade. With the coming of the railways the coach trade died away but Broadway became a popular stopping-off point for exploration of the Cotswolds.

Broadway Tower This distinctive feature is built on the site of an ancient beacon and is said to have inspired JRR Tolkien to create the tower of Amon Hen and the Hill of Seeing in *The Lord of the Rings*. The tower is one of the country's premier viewpoints; on a clear day it is possible to see 13 counties and enjoy views of the Vale of Evesham, the Vale of Gloucester, the Severn valley and the Welsh mountains.

Stanton This is essentially a single street village claimed by many to be one of the oldest in the Cotswolds. Most of the houses date from the 17th century but the village was extensively restored by the architect Sir Philip Stott after he purchased large tracts of it just before the First World War.

Laverton A large hamlet located beneath the Cotswold edge, Laverton contains several substantial and well-built farmhouses that date back to the 16th century and make good use of local stone. Laverton is close to the Cotswold Way and the many fine views in the area make it popular with walkers. Broadway to the north and Stanton to the south are within easy reach.

Stanway The village of Stanway is dominated by the gate-house to Stanway House where a mixture of Gothic, Renaissance and Dutch styles are given a pleasing unity by the local stone. Stanway House was built during the 1580s on the site of an earlier manor house. It is mostly Jacobean in style and has a remarkable 60-pane oriel window. The grounds contain a restored water garden which features the highest fountain in England, an impressive tithe barn dating from 1370 and a log-fired brewing house. The church of St Peter retains its Jacobean pulpit but has suffered badly at the hands of Victorian restorers.

Burford The eastern gateway to the Cotswolds, Burford built its reputation on wool, quarrying and coaching. Wool was important from the 14th century onwards and the stone from quarries near the town was used in the construction of some of Britain's finest buildings, ranging from Blenheim Palace to St Paul's Cathedral. Burford's heyday as a coaching town came in the 18th century when it was an important stop on routes into Oxford and London; "Burford Bait", the huge meals served by the inns, were famous

locally. Burford's steep high street with its many inns is well-known. The church is interesting both architecturally and historically. In the interior a carving includes the first representation of Amazonian Indians in England and the font preserves the autograph of a Leveller prisoner held in the church during the Civil War.

Minster Lovell Minster combines an idyllic rural setting with buildings and ruins that reflect the village's interesting and varied past. A bridge across the Windrush leads to the High Street which has a well-balanced selection of thatched cottages and other Cotswold stone houses. St Kenelm's church was built in 1431 and has an attractive vaulted ceiling underneath the central tower. Some of the stained glass may be original and there is a fine alabaster

knight's tomb, probably that of William, the seventh Baron of Lovell, who built the church and manor house; the house dates from 1435. Colourful local legends surround the fate of the ninth Lord Lovell who fought with Richard III at Bosworth Field and became involved in the Lambert Simnel rebellion, after which he disappeared. According to these stories, building work in the early 18th century revealed an underground vault complete with skeleton. In the mid-18th century the manor was dismantled to provide stone for nearby farm buildings. Also worth noting is the round medieval dovecote.

Bourton-on-the-Water

Five ornamental bridges span the river Windrush in Bourton-on-the-Water giving it a unique appeal and the nickname of the "Venice of the Cotswolds". Moving downstream, the five bridges are: Bourton Bridge, built in 1806 and widened in 1959; Mill Bridge (also known as Broad Bridge) built in 1654 on the site of a former ford; High Bridge, a footbridge built in 1756; New Bridge (or Moore Bridge) built in 1911 to traverse another ford; and Coronation Bridge, built in 1953 to replace an 18th-century wooden bridge. During the summer a game of football is attempted between two of the bridges. The goal-posts are set in the river and teams play using a standard football. The aim of the game is to score as many goals as possible but the general effect is to get everyone else as wet as possible!

Bourton-on-the-Water is served by the church of St Lawrence. The only visible part of the old church is the chancel, built in 1328 by Walter de Burhton. In 1784 the Norman church was largely replaced with today's neo-Classical style building with its thick tower housing a clock and bells. Further additions were made in the 1870s when the present nave was constructed. The nave roof is a fine example of a king-post roof.

Stroud Five valleys come together at Stroud making it a natural centre for trade and transport. In the Middle Ages Stroud established itself as a centre of the cloth industry and at the height of its prosperity there were 150 cloth mills in and around the town. Stroud was famous for manufacturing the cloth used in military uniforms. The centre of Stroud reflects its role as a market town with many narrow streets, a Tudor town hall and the Shambles, an area for butchers.

Miserden Most of the buildings in Miserden are 19th and 20th century in origin but the village has had a long history of growth, decay and renewal. Near to the village are the earthworks of a motte and bailey castle which was erected shortly after the Norman Conquest. The name Miserden is a corruption of the name of the family, la Musarder, that held the manor from the 12th century onwards. Among the surviving 17th-century houses are the rectory, Lampacre cottage and a pair of cottages, one of which used to be the blacksmith's.

Painswick The stream below Painswick once provided power for its woollen mills whilst its crystal clear water made the village an important centre for cloth dyeing. Many of the houses in the village date from the 17th and 18th centuries and once belonged to wealthy wool merchants. At the centre of the village is the parish church of St Mary's, with its fine churchyard and beautiful yew trees.

Bath This is a famous city that has had two major heydays. The first was during the Roman occupation when the town of *Aqua Sulis* grew up around the natural hot springs in the area and the second was during the Regency and Georgian periods when the craze for taking the waters made Bath the centre of fashion. Substantial traces of both periods can still be seen in the city today. The city is on the very edge of the Cotswolds and the stone in this area is usually described as creamy rather than golden. The Roman temple and baths, the abbey and the city's famous crescents are all built from locally quarried limestone.

Apart from the Roman baths and the temple, the ancient city of Bath largely disappeared during the Saxon period and the city was mainly in royal and monastic hands throughout the Middle Ages. The spa trade began to revive after the Dissolution of the Monasteries but it was not until after the Civil War that Bath began to be a health centre for the aristocracy. The new Bath was largely built in the Classical style with long stretches of identical façades to give impressions of palatial scale and Classical decorum. The shop housing Sally Lunn's tea room is the oldest house in Bath dating from 1482.

Castle Combe Although it is well to the south of the traditional Cotswold area, Castle Combe displays many of the charms of the area and is a popular destination for visitors. The village is centred on a market cross that reflects its growth through wool trading. The village is situated on the By Brook and a pretty bridge spans the stream here. The Norman castle that gives the village its name has largely disappeared but the castle mound still exists.

44

The photogenic charm of the village has regularly attracted film-makers. In 1966 a section of the By Brook near the bridge was converted into a miniature port complete with jetty and boats for the filming of *Dr Doolittle*. There are many fine walks in the area and the village is on the Macmillan Way long-distance footpath. The disused RAF airfield is now the home of the Castle Combe motor-racing circuit.

North Nibley This small village lies between Wotton-under-Edge and Dursley. The last battle between private armies fought on English soil took place at Nibley Green on March 20 1469. Above the village, on Nibley Knoll, stands the Tyndale Monument. Named after William Tyndale, a translator of the New Testament, this dramatic 111ft (34m) high tower was built in 1866 using stone from Hampton quarry, near Stroud.